The GROSSEST Bug Activity Book EVER!

W0081689

little bigfoot
an imprint of sasquatch books
seattle, wa

Copyright © 2025 by LITTLE BIGFOOT

All rights reserved. No portion of this book may be
reproduced or utilized in any form, or by any electronic, mechanical,
or other means, without the prior written permission of the publisher.

Printed in Colombia

LITTLE BIGFOOT with colophon is a registered
trademark of Blue Star Press, LLC

9 8 7 6 5 4 3 2 1

The authorized representative in the
EU for product safety and compliance is
Authorised Rep Compliance Ltd., Ground Floor,
71 Lower Baggot Street, Dublin D02 P593, Ireland.
www.arccompliance.com

A catalog record for this book is available from the
Library of Congress upon request.

Produced by One+One Books

Design by Will Mack
Text by L.J. Tracosas
Copyedit by Laura Whittemore
Proofread by Carrie Wicks
Photo research by Micah Schmidt

ISBN: 978-1-63217-629-5

Sasquatch Books
1325 Fourth Avenue, Suite 1025
Seattle, WA 98101

SasquatchBooks.com

Contents

Slimy, Stinky, Icky, Gooey, Creepy-Crawly BUGS!

What is it about bugs that's just *so* **gross**? Is it because of their tickly little feet? Is it because some are so **slimy**, **hairy**, or **gooey**? Is it because they make us jump when we find them in our house or, worse, **our food**?

Whatever it is that's gross about bugs—the bugs in this book take it to a whole new level. Think ants are gross? What about ants that smell like **rotting fruit**?!

Do **spiders** creep you out? What about ones that are as big as your face?!

Think nothing could be more **disgusting** than lice? What about a bug that hangs out in its own spittle?!

EW, SO GROSS!

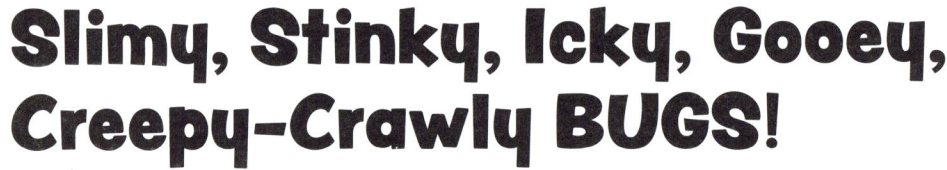

4

Welcome to the Big, Wide, and Totally Disgusting World of Bugs!

Scientists estimate that there are more than 10 quintillion bugs in the world. That means that for every *one* person on the planet you can count, there are about 1 billion bugs! Bugs live on every continent except Antarctica.

And bugs have been around for a long time. Some date back 400 million years. Over all that time, bugs have evolved different ways to survive in the world— and sometimes those ways are really, really gross. From eating poop to spraying stuff out of their butts, bugs can be pretty unpleasant. Just how unpleasant? Turn the page to really get gross.

So What *Is* Gross?

Here are some of the most unpleasant qualities that make bugs gross!

Creepy OK, some bugs creep you out just by the look of them. Long antennae? Icky, long legs? Big pincers? *shudder*

Stinky Do you smell something? It might be one of the thousands of bugs that use yucky stink to protect themselves. Rotting coconut? Burning rubber? P.U.!

Crawly Have you ever felt a tickle on your arm and looked to find a bug skittering on you? All those sticky, prickly legs . . . Ewwww.

Slimy Ooey, gooey, sticky, icky slime is just SO disgusting.

Hairy You might be able to handle a small house spider. But what about a big, hairy tarantula?

Huge You may love bugs, but do you still love them when they're as big as your thumb or your whole hand? How about if they are big enough to EAT a mouse?

SICKENING SCALE

How slimy, creepy, stinky is this bug?
Color in your rating.

CREEPY

STINKY

CRAWLY

SLIMY

HAIRY

HUGE

Throughout this book, you'll find **Sickening Scales** and **Gross-Out Meters**. This is where you get to rank exactly how disgusting you think each bug is. For the Sickening Scale, color in how creepy, stinky, crawly, slimy, hairy, or huge you think each bug is. For the Gross-Out Meter, rate their overall grossness. Think they're just a little icky? Only color in one box. Is it the grossest thing you've ever seen? Color in everything!

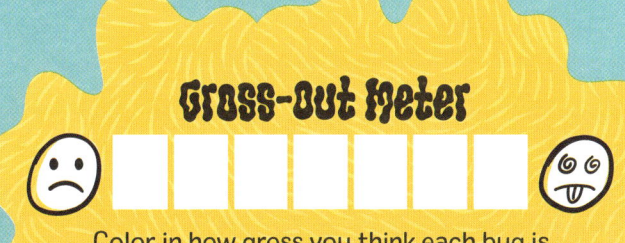

Gross-Out Meter

Color in how gross you think each bug is.

Insect or Not an Insect?

So what's a bug? People use the word *bug* to mean any little creepy-crawly with legs, so in this book we will too! All bugs are insects, but not all insects are bugs.

What makes an insect an insect? Scientifically speaking, all insects are invertebrates, meaning they don't have a bony spine. Insects also share these features:

Two antennae

Head

Thorax

Three pairs of legs (six legs total)

Abdomen

Usually one or two pairs of wings (though some true insects, like silverfish, are wingless)

Pop Quiz: Who's a Real Insect?

Test your insect knowledge with this quiz: Who is a real insect? Circle your answer!

Banana Slug

Definitely an insect!   No way is that an insect!

Ant

Definitely an insect!   No way is that an insect!

Wasp

Definitely an insect!   No way is that an insect!

Butterfly

Definitely an insect!   No way is that an insect!

Caterpillar

Definitely an insect!   No way is that an insect!

Daddy Longlegs

Definitely an insect!   No way is that an insect!

Spider

Definitely an insect!   No way is that an insect!

Glowworm

Definitely an insect!   No way is that an insect!

Walking Stick

Definitely an insect!   No way is that an insect!

Bugs Near Me!

OK, don't freak out. But right now you're surrounded by tons of bugs. Just outside your door, there are about **2,000 insects**. In your house, there are likely hundreds. Some you can see, and many you can't. Experts estimate that there are **10 quintillion** (that's 10,000,000,000,000,000,000) insects on Earth—that's a lot of insects!

Bug Safari

Grab a magnifying glass, if you have one, and go on a bug safari to get to know the bugs near you. Circle all the bugs you can find. (And when you find them, look but don't touch!)

What's the grossest bug you've found near you?

Gnat

Wasp

Fly

Grasshopper

Stink Bug

Moth

Honeybee

Butterfly

Ant

Praying Mantis

Pill Bug

Cricket

What's That Smell?

STINK BUG

Stink bugs don't always smell bad. But when they are threatened (or squished), they let out a stinky spray.

Some species of stink bugs can even **shoot the spray** a few inches away. You can find them in 38 states, and you might recognize them as **visitors to your home**. Stink bugs like to come indoors in the winter and can often be found strolling along walls and ceilings. But don't worry! They won't stink up the place unless you **bother** them.

SICKENING SCALE

How slimy, creepy, stinky is this bug?
Color in your rating.

CREEPY ✿ ✿ ✿ ✿ ✿
STINKY ✿ ✿ ✿ ✿ ✿
CRAWLY ✿ ✿ ✿ ✿ ✿
SLIMY ✿ ✿ ✿ ✿ ✿
HAIRY ✿ ✿ ✿ ✿ ✿
HUGE ✿ ✿ ✿ ✿ ✿

Just How Bad Does a Stink Bug Stink?

Have you ever smelled a stink bug's stink? Some people say it smells like cilantro, a cooking herb; others say it's like burnt rubber; still others think it smells like rotten meat. How bad do you think those smell? Color in each Stink-o-Meter for smelly things, then compare it to the stink bug rating.

Stink Bug

Trash

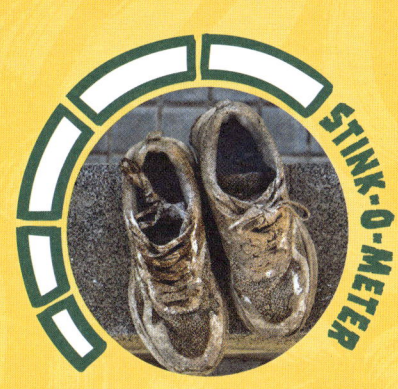

Smelly Sneakers

Wet Dog

Circle the stinkiest thing on this page!

Spoiled Milk

Skunk

Draw your own stinky thing!

Bombs Away!

BOMBARDIER BEETLE

When you're a tiny bug in a big world, almost anything can eat you.

That's why some **bombardier beetles** have a powerful defense: a burning-hot, gooey spray that **explodes** from their butt! Inside the bombardier beetle's abdomen are chambers holding two liquids. When the beetle is attacked, it mixes the liquids together and creates the **super-hot spray**. In some species of bombardier beetle, the substance creates a foam that's toxic to predators.

Gross-Out Meter

Color in how gross you think this bug is.

Head-to-Head

Who do you think would win in a matchup between the bombardier beetle and these potential predators?

VS

VS

VS

BIRD

With sharp, pointed beaks, birds—and especially quail—spear insects for their meals. Can the beetle avoid becoming dinner?

WINNER: _____

ANT

Strong and quick foes, ants usually attack in groups. Do you think the beetle could win?

WINNER: _____

TOAD

Much bigger than the bombardier beetle, a toad hides until prey comes along. Then, surprise! They can swallow their food whole. Does the beetle have any chance of surviving?

WINNER: _____

For the Love of Poop!
DUNG BEETLE

Rollers roll their dung away from the poop pile in as straight a line as possible following the **SUN**. If it's nighttime? They follow the **MOON** or the **MILKY WAY**.

Lots of insects are very into poop. But while flies may swarm around a stinky pile, *dung* (another word for poop) beetles dig right in.

In fact, dung beetles are **born in poop**. Their parents lay their eggs there. For these bugs, poop also makes a healthy meal—that's right: they *eat* poop. But not all species of dung beetle enjoy their poop meals the same way. **Rollers** pull off a piece of poop, form it into a ball, and roll it away to store and enjoy later. **Tunnelers** dig down through the pile and burrow underneath it, so they can pick off bits of poop whenever they want to. Finally, **dwellers** . . . well, they live in and eat the dung.

SICKENING SCALE
How slimy, creepy, stinky is this bug?
Color in your rating.

CREEPY ✿ ✿ ✿ ✿ ✿
STINKY ✿ ✿ ✿ ✿ ✿
CRAWLY ✿ ✿ ✿ ✿ ✿
SLIMY ✿ ✿ ✿ ✿ ✿
HAIRY ✿ ✿ ✿ ✿ ✿
HUGE ✿ ✿ ✿ ✿ ✿

Roll Away

Be a roller and follow the sun to get to the perfect spot where you can enjoy your poop in peace. Watch out for predators and dead ends!

Little Bit of Spittle

SPITTLEBUG

Have you ever seen a gob of frothy spit on a leaf and thought *Gross! Who would spit there?*

Well, you probably saw a young spittlebug, called a **nymph**. As the growing nymphs eat plants, **sap** oozes out of their butts. That sap mixes with their bodily fluids to create foamy bubbles around them, which help hide the nymphs from predators and keep them cool and wet in the heat. When spittlebugs grow up, they're sometimes called **froghoppers** because of their impressive jumps.

Gross-Out Meter

Color in how gross you think this bug is.

Your Own Gross Bug

Make up a gross bug name. (Maybe fart fly? Smelly belly button ant?) Then try this fill-in-the-blank activity to create a bug with mysterious and gross things coming out of them.

Have you ever seen a/n _____ in _____?
               gross thing   a place

Congratulations, you saw a_____bug.
                      your gross bug name

They create _____ by _____ing and _____ing.
            gross thing   action   action

The _____ comes out of their _____.
     gross thing   body part

_____ bugs live in _____ and love to
 your gross bug name   place

go to _____. Can you believe it? It really is a _____
       another place   description

world of bugs!

Draw a picture of your gross bug here:

Pick from the following words:

GROSS THING: dung, spit, puke, dirt, hair, garbage, rotten food

PLACE: the grass, a house, a yard, the water, a barn, school, after-school care, the store

BODY PART: eye, butt, stomach, mouth, nose

ACTION: dancing, eating, pooping, puking, drinking, sleeping, hiding

DESCRIPTION: scary, funny, creepy, gross, weird, beautiful, confusing

They're Actually Kind of Sweet

EARWIG

Meet the earwig! You might have heard that they wriggle into your ears at night and nibble on your brain. But that's not true.

SICKENING SCALE

How slimy, creepy, stinky is this bug?
Color in your rating.

CREEPY	✿	✿	✿	✿	✿
STINKY	✿	✿	✿	✿	✿
CRAWLY	✿	✿	✿	✿	✿
SLIMY	✿	✿	✿	✿	✿
HAIRY	✿	✿	✿	✿	✿
HUGE	✿	✿	✿	✿	✿

These creepy-crawlies are actually **helpful for gardens**—earwigs eat other insects that can damage gardens, and they help make good soil. Female earwigs are also **good moms**—aww. Unlike most bug moms, they care for their eggs, cleaning them and keeping them together. Once the baby earwigs, sometimes also called **wiglets**, are born, the mom wigs feed them till they are big enough to take care of themselves. So sweet!

Good Stuff

Match these creepy-crawlies to the helpful/good/nice fact about them.

HOVERFLIES

HERDER ANTS

HOUSE CENTIPEDES

HOUSE SPIDERS

These insects protect aphids from predators. In exchange, the aphids feed them a sugary substance called honeydew.

These creepy-crawlies spin webs to catch mosquitoes, cockroaches, and wasps.

These many-legged hunters feast on pests in your pantry.

These yellow jacket look-alikes don't sting and are also great pollinators.

How Big Is That Beetle?

HERCULES BEETLE

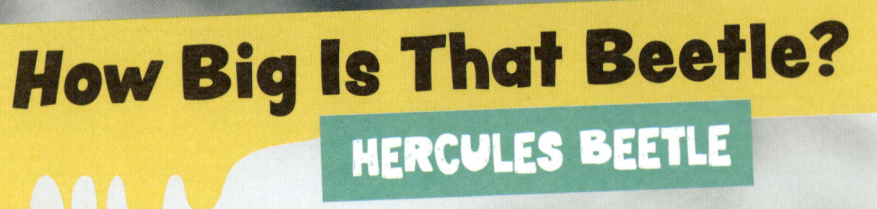

Hercules beetles were named for the **STRONG MAN** from Greek mythology.

Picture a slimy, wriggly grub the size of a sausage and you have the super-gross larval stage of the Hercules beetle.

Instead of spinning a cocoon, the Hercules beetle larva builds a **container out of its poop** and crawls inside. And instead of emerging as a beautiful butterfly, a sharp-horned **battle bug** crawls out of the container, ready to fight for territory. Luckily, the adult male beetle isn't half as gross as the larvae because it is one of the longest bugs in the world, measuring up to **7 inches** (17.8 cm) long.

Gross-Out Meter

:(▢▢▢▢▢▢▢ @_@

Color in how gross you think this bug is.

All Grown-Up

Match each insect larva to its grown-up stage.

Though they begin their lives as white wormlike larvae, these insects grow up to be black or reddish brown.

Hoverfly

These hairy larvae grow up to be snug bugs in rugs.

Black Ant

Rat-tailed maggots get their name because of their tails.

Carpet Beetle

Grown, these flies look like another insect.

Drone Fly

Don't Freak Out!
CAMEL SPIDER

Here's one of the creepiest crawlies ever: giant, fast, and with a very weird way of eating their prey.

Also known as a **WIND SCORPION**, these creepers race along at speeds of about 10 miles per hour.

The camel spider thrives in the desert. It's big for a bug, measuring about 6 inches long. Though it's an **arachnid**, it's not really a spider; rather, it's a creature called a **solpugid**, related to mites and scorpions. It looks like it has 10 legs, but 2 are extra sensory parts called **pedipalps**.

One thing that makes them super creepy is their **giant jaws** that move up and down and side to side. Fortunately, they're not venomous, so they can't hurt people. But that doesn't help their prey (which are sometimes as big as they are!), which they eat by injecting stuff to dissolve their insides, which they then suck out **like a delicious milkshake**!

SICKENING SCALE

How slimy, creepy, stinky is this bug?
Color in your rating.

CREEPY ✿ ✿ ✿ ✿ ✿

STINKY ✿ ✿ ✿ ✿ ✿

CRAWLY ✿ ✿ ✿ ✿ ✿

SLIMY ✿ ✿ ✿ ✿ ✿

HAIRY ✿ ✿ ✿ ✿ ✿

HUGE ✿ ✿ ✿ ✿ ✿

Build-a-Bug

Build the most dreadful bug you can think of from these weird insect parts.

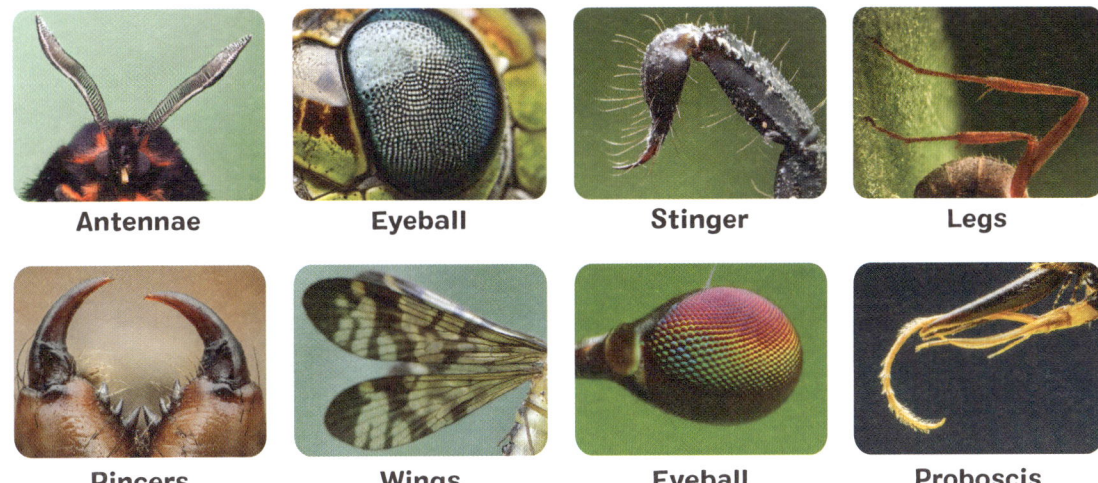

| Antennae | Eyeball | Stinger | Legs |
| Pincers | Wings | Eyeball | Proboscis |

Draw your bug in the space below:

Write a description of how it uses its gross features:

Hairy and Scary

TARANTULA

Why is it that hair makes everything just a little more gross?

So, what's creepier than a spider? A hairy spider, of course! Extra points if they have fangs and venom! There are about **900 species** of tarantulas living on every continent except Antarctica. Some are small, about as big as a fingernail. Others are **as big as a dinner plate**. These spiders live underground, so you won't get caught in a tarantula web. Tarantulas are excellent hunters, sensing prey through vibrations and **pouncing to attack**. Then they sink their fangs into their meal and inject venom.

SICKENING SCALE

How slimy, creepy, stinky is this bug?
Color in your rating.

CREEPY ✿ ✿ ✿ ✿ ✿
STINKY ✿ ✿ ✿ ✿ ✿
CRAWLY ✿ ✿ ✿ ✿ ✿
SLIMY ✿ ✿ ✿ ✿ ✿
HAIRY ✿ ✿ ✿ ✿ ✿
HUGE ✿ ✿ ✿ ✿ ✿

Mealtime!

Connect the dots to reveal something that tarantulas eat.

1
2
3
4
5
6
7
8
9
10
11
12
13
14
15
16
17
18
19
20
21
22
23
24
25
26
27
28
29
30
31
32
33
34
35
36
37
38
39
40
41
42
43
44
45
46
47
48
49
50
51
52
53
54
55
56
57
58
59
60
61
62
63
64
65
66
67
68
69
70
71
72
73
74
75
76
77
78

Caterpillar or...Alien?

MONKEY SLUG CATERPILLAR

Meet the monkey slug caterpillar! It looks like a blob monster that might live under your bed. It's actually the weird, hairy, sucker-footed larva of the hag moth.

They have **nine "arms,"** which aren't arms at all: they're just wavy body parts that help the monkey slug caterpillar hide among fallen leaves to avoid being eaten. If a **predator** does happen to bite an arm? It breaks off, and the caterpillar survives.

Gross-Out Meter

Color in how gross you think this bug is.

Monkey Slug What??

Now create your own yucky, wacky, weirdo bug name!

STEP 1. Pick the letter your first name starts with:

A/B/C	Purple
D/E/F	Orange
G/H/I	Green
J/K/L	Red
M/N/O	Rainbow
P/Q/R	Silver
S/T/U	Brown
V/W/X	Pink
Y/Z/other	Blue

STEP 2. Find your birth month:

January	Slimy
February	Stinky
March	Oily
April	Hairy
May	Bumpy
June	Scaly
July	Funky
August	Spitty
September	Smelly
October	Lumpy
November	Yucky
December	Oozy

What's the **WEIRDEST** caterpillar you've ever seen? What do you think it transformed into?

STEP 3. Find your birth date:

1	Kitten		17	Bat
2	Falcon		18	Bear
3	Newt		19	Owl
4	Raccoon		20	Hummingbird
5	Snake		21	Otter
6	Lemur		22	Shark
7	Turkey		23	Ostrich
8	Hippo		24	Mongoose
9	Fish		25	Zebra
10	Cheetah		26	Buzzard
11	Puppy		27	Vulture
12	Crow		28	Mouse
13	Salamander		29	Deer
14	Caterpillar		30	Lion
15	Rhinoceros		31	Lamb
16	Llama			

STEP 4. Now the first letter of your last name:

A/B/C	Moth
D/E/F	Spider
G/H/I	Fly
J/K/L	Cricket
M/N/O	Flea
P/Q/R	Mite
S/T/U	Bee
V/W/X	Beetle
Y/Z/other	Termite

If your name is Joe Smith and your birthday is August 1, your bug's name is:

Red Spitty Kitten Bee

The Crawliest of Creepies

MILLIPEDE

These bugs aren't true insects. They're related to **LOBSTERS** and **SHRIMP**.

These wormlike bugs give most people the heebie-jeebies thanks to their tons of creepy feet.

The word *millipede* comes from the Latin words *mille,* which means "**thousand**," and *ped*, which means "**foot**." But millipedes don't really have 1,000 feet—they usually have more like 24 to 750. In fact, the only true millipede (thousand feet!) was discovered in 2021 in Western Australia. *Eumillipes persephone* (that's the millipede's scientific name, in Latin) has **1,306 legs**, and is less than 4 inches long (10 cm). It was found nearly 197 feet (60 m) underground.

SICKENING SCALE

How slimy, creepy, stinky is this bug? Color in your rating.

CREEPY

STINKY

CRAWLY

SLIMY

HAIRY

HUGE

Guess the Legs on the Millipede

Guess how many legs each millipede has! Here's a clue: Millipedes have two pairs of legs per body segment. Write your guess at the bottom of each image.

Tractor Millipede: _____

Red Millipede: _____

Flat-Backed Millipede: _____

Giant Pill Millipede: _____

Giant Millipede: _____

Pink Dragon Millipede: _____

Deadly Gross

ASSASSIN BUG

Assassin bugs have a **SMALL HEAD** that looks connected to their body by a **THIN NECK**.

Assassin bugs are great hunters, but they're kind of gross eaters.

They're **built for attack**: These bugs have long front legs that they use to grab and hold their prey—usually flying insects—and a **piercing proboscis** (a tubelike mouth) they stick into the prey. Then they inject a **toxin** that turns their target's **insides to goo**. That same piercing proboscis then acts like a straw, which the bug uses to slurp up its meal. Yum!

While assassin bugs aren't usually dangerous to humans, they have painful bites and can carry disease, so **keep your distance**.

SICKENING SCALE

How slimy, creepy, stinky is this bug? Color in your rating.

CREEPY	✿	✿	✿	✿	✿
STINKY	✿	✿	✿	✿	✿
CRAWLY	✿	✿	✿	✿	✿
SLIMY	✿	✿	✿	✿	✿
HAIRY	✿	✿	✿	✿	✿
HUGE	✿	✿	✿	✿	✿

Artful Assassins

There are thousands of different kinds of assassin bugs around the world. Get inspired by these examples and then color in the assassin bugs below!

Orange Assassin Bug

Flower Assassin Bug

Bee Assassin Bug

Did That Stick Just Move?

STICK AND LEAF BUGS

Imagine finding a cool stick or leaf on the ground but when you reach for it, you realize it has *eyes* and it's *looking at you*?

Lots of bugs are **camouflaged** to blend into their surroundings, but some take it to a whole new level. Stick bugs are disguised as just another stick, and some can be up to **12 inches (30.4 cm) long**. You'd never know you just walked by a giant bug—unless you tried to pick it up! The Australian walking stick blends into the forest floor by resembling a stick, but if it curls its tail, it looks like a dead leaf too.

Speaking of leaves, there are also **leaf insects**, which look more like leaves than bugs! Some have markings that look like holes or tears in leaves, and some even sway in the breeze like a real leaf.

Nothing to see here!

Gross-Out Meter

:([ ][ ][ ][ ][ ][ ][ ] @@

Color in how gross you think this bug is.

Seek-a-Stick

Can you find the camouflaged bugs in the photos below?

Don't Let the Bedbugs Bite

BEDBUG

What could be worse than flat little bugs that hide in your mattress during the day and crawl out to drink your blood at night? Gross!

If you squish a bedbug, it gives off a musty, sweet smell kind of like a **STINK BUG**.

And once they've infested a house, getting rid of them is a full-time job. They don't just live in mattresses but also inhabit the corners of wooden and fabric-covered furniture, light sockets, and anywhere else they can fit their tiny bodies. Bedbug bites leave clusters of **itchy bumps** and are a telltale sign you might have some nighttime visitors (although not everyone reacts to them).

Looking for some possible protection? **The color of your pj's might help**: One study showed that bedbugs are drawn to red and black, but they're less drawn to yellow and green. Bedbugs get hungry between midnight and 5 a.m., when you're deep asleep. So **sleep tight!**

SICKENING SCALE

How slimy, creepy, stinky is this bug?
Color in your rating.

CREEPY ✿ ✿ ✿ ✿ ✿

STINKY ✿ ✿ ✿ ✿ ✿

CRAWLY ✿ ✿ ✿ ✿ ✿

SLIMY ✿ ✿ ✿ ✿ ✿

HAIRY ✿ ✿ ✿ ✿ ✿

HUGE ✿ ✿ ✿ ✿ ✿

Bedbug or Impostor?

Bedbugs are commonly confused with other household pests. Identify the similarities and differences between a true bedbug and its look-alikes.

Spider Beetle

Tick

What's alike? _____

What's different? _____

What's alike? _____

What's different? _____

Cockroach Nymph

Carpet Beetle

What's alike? _____

What's different? _____

What's alike? _____

What's different? _____

Unwanted Visitors
WEEVILS

Have you ever opened up a box of cereal . . . and the cereal moves?!

That may just be the very worst way to meet a bug! Rice weevils, maize weevils, and wheat weevils are frequent pantry visitors, but it's a wide world of weevils! Easy to identify because of their **long snout**, a weevil is a type of beetle that lives across the globe on every continent but Antarctica.

There are **95,000** species of weevils. Some are known for their interesting features, like **giraffe weevils**, which have long necks.

I'm a giraffe weevil!

Gross-Out Meter

Color in how gross you think this bug is.

How Many Weevils?

Seek and find 10 weevils in these pantry foods they're known to infest. Some clues? Here are signs of weevils: little holes in storage boxes or bags, oddly colored food items, and little white specks (which might be weevil eggs).

Slime to Survive

PEAR SLUG

Look at me, all grown-up!

Here's a bug you don't want to cuddle!

The **pear slug** is not really a slug. Instead, it's the **larva of the sawfly**. They're often mistaken for slugs because of their ooey-gooey appearance. Even though they're truly yellow, they appear dark green or black because they slather their bodies in liquid slime, which is actually **their own waste**. You might be thinking *Yuck!* Predators think the same, so that slime can help the pear slug survive. When the pear slug is ready, it drops down to the ground from the leaves where it had been living, and then transforms into the **pear sawfly**, a shiny black fly that looks like a wasp.

SICKENING SCALE
How slimy, creepy, stinky is this bug?
Color in your rating.

CREEPY ✿ ✿ ✿ ✿ ✿
STINKY ✿ ✿ ✿ ✿ ✿
CRAWLY ✿ ✿ ✿ ✿ ✿
SLIMY ✿ ✿ ✿ ✿ ✿
HAIRY ✿ ✿ ✿ ✿ ✿
HUGE ✿ ✿ ✿ ✿ ✿

Follow That Slime

Follow the pear slug's slime trail to see where it's been.

Examine Exoskeletons

BUG MOLTS

Have you ever happened upon a bug only to discover that the bug isn't actually . . . in there?

No, it's not a **zombie bug** carcass. You've found a **bug molt**. Many bugs have hard exoskeletons that protect them like a shell. That shell isn't flexible like your skin, so when the bug grows, the exoskeleton can't stretch with them. So the bug grows a new **exoskeleton** underneath the old one, the old one splits open, and the bug crawls out and leaves the molted exoskeleton behind for you to find. Take **cicadas**, for example. Young cicadas, or **nymphs**, live underground and then crawl out as they get older. (OK, you're

right, they might be zombies!) Underneath the exoskeleton "skin," the nymph is growing its adult body, which looks completely different—and has wings. It takes them a few hours to crack out of the old exoskeleton.

Gross-Out Meter

Color in how gross you think this bug is.

Match a Molt!

Match the bug to its molted exoskeleton.

Dragonfly Larva

Cicada

Damselfly

Grasshopper

Roach Riddles
COCKROACH

Cockroaches have skittered around Earth for more than **120 MILLION YEARS**.

There are 4,500 species of roaches in the world . . .

But only about 30 are considered truly gross pests, and just 4 regularly make their way into homes and restaurants—the German, American, oriental, and brown-banded cockroaches. Why are they gross? Those cockroaches are **covered in germs**, and there's even more bacteria in their guts. They carry 33 types of **bacteria** and 6 **parasites**. So if they walk or poop on something you put in your mouth, you could get sick. Plus, cockroaches often come in groups. If you see one, there are likely dozens more. And they just have that ick factor, don't they?

SICKENING SCALE
How slimy, creepy, stinky is this bug?
Color in your rating.

CREEPY ✿ ✿ ✿ ✿ ✿
STINKY ✿ ✿ ✿ ✿ ✿
CRAWLY ✿ ✿ ✿ ✿ ✿
SLIMY ✿ ✿ ✿ ✿ ✿
HAIRY ✿ ✿ ✿ ✿ ✿
HUGE ✿ ✿ ✿ ✿ ✿

Cockroach Scramble!

Meet just a few of the thousands of cockroach species living among humans. Unscramble their names below to find out more.

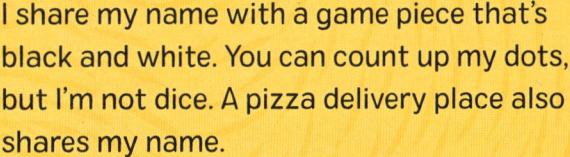

I share my name with a game piece that's black and white. You can count up my dots, but I'm not dice. A pizza delivery place also shares my name.

DOMION COCKROACH _____

I get pretty mad when I'm trying to protect my space from invaders. I get pushy and stand tall. But what really scares them away? I make a sound like a snake or a mad cat—and that's where I get my name.

HSINSGI COCKROACH _____

Even though my name might make you think I come from Down Under, I'm actually right at home in the southeastern United States. Sometimes I'm also called a shad roach.

ARSUIANTLI COCKROACH _____

I'm named for the skeleton shape on my noggin and my spooky coloring.

DHAETS **H**DEA COCKROACH

_____ _____

Slimy Night-Lights!

GLOWWORM

The **BRIGHTER** the glow, the **HUNGRIER** the worm!

Mmmmm, midges . . .

Imagine you're a tiny bug flying through a cave guided by a soft blue-green glow.

Sounds kind of like a Disney ride, right? That is, until you're caught in dangling sticky strings of silk dotted with droplets of **mucus-like pee** (yes, pee)—and then you're eaten by a squirmy little larva. Ugh.

That's the fate of millions of midges in certain caves in New Zealand. That light comes from thousands of glowworms (the larval stage of **fungus gnats**—still gross!). Glowworms like warm, soggy, and wet places, like damp caves.

Their glow is thanks to *bioluminescence*, the ability of some creatures to give off light. In the glowworms' case, they're able to produce a chemical reaction in a **special light organ in their butts**.

Gross-Out Meter

Color in how gross you think this bug is.

46

Glowworm Grows Up

Fill in the crossword using the clues below.

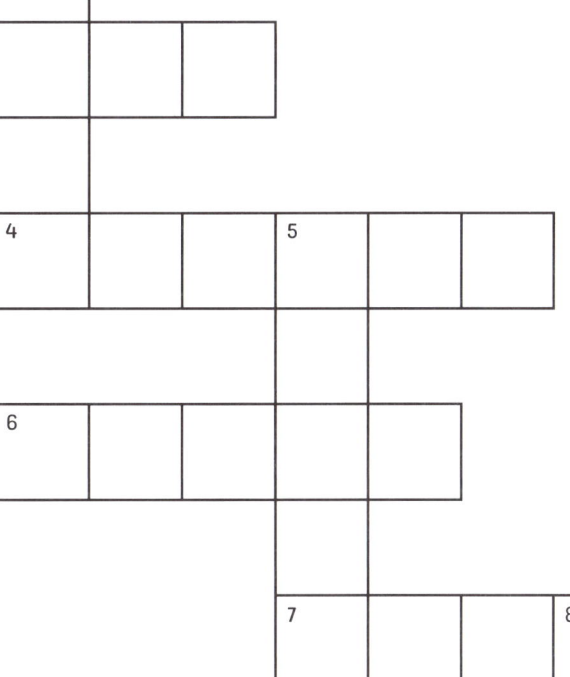

ACROSS

3. If a glowworm is really bright, it's really _____.

4. What glowworm strings feel like.

6. Another word for a baby bug.

7. Another word for *wet*.

DOWN

1. The bugs that glowworms eat.

2. The part of a glowworm that lights up.

5. One place glowworms are found.

8. Bioluminescence is how these bugs _____.

Bird Poop Disguise

BIRD POOP CATERPILLAR

osmeterium

From poop to pretty!

Bird poop caterpillars have found a great way to avoid being eaten by birds.

We'll give you one guess! That's right: They disguise themselves as bird poop.

Not surprisingly, birds aren't very interested in their own poop, so bird poop caterpillars can just lounge on leaves, hiding in plain sight. If a predator does decide to take a closer look, the caterpillar sticks out its **osmeterium**, a hidden body part that looks like **bright-red horns**, to scare them away. The bird poop caterpillar eventually transforms into the beautiful black-and-yellow **giant swallowtail**, one of the largest butterflies in the United States.

SICKENING SCALE

How slimy, creepy, stinky is this bug? Color in your rating.

CREEPY
STINKY
CRAWLY
SLIMY
HAIRY
HUGE

Who Becomes Who?

Match the caterpillar to its moth or butterfly!

I get my moth name from the moonlike spots on my wings.

Black Swallowtail

After metamorphosis, I'm named for the shape of my hind wings, which look like a bird's tail feathers.

Cecropia Moth

Some people also call me a woolly slug, but my moth name uses another fabric.

Luna Moth

I become the biggest moth in North America!

Southern Flannel Moth

Little Stinkers

STINK ANTS

Stink ants get their name from the smell they give off when bothered.

If one stink ant smells rotten, can you imagine how **BAD** a **WHOLE COLONY** of them smells?

SICKENING SCALE

How slimy, creepy, stinky is this bug?
Color in your rating.

CREEPY ✿ ✿ ✿ ✿ ✿

STINKY ✿ ✿ ✿ ✿ ✿

CRAWLY ✿ ✿ ✿ ✿ ✿

SLIMY ✿ ✿ ✿ ✿ ✿

HAIRY ✿ ✿ ✿ ✿ ✿

HUGE ✿ ✿ ✿ ✿ ✿

Some people think it smells like **rotten coconut**, and others think of **stinky cheese**. Outside, stink ants, also known as odorous house ants, look for sugary food, often eating **aphid poop** (also called honeydew—now that's a nice name for something really gross!). But sometimes, they find their way inside, marching in a line toward any tasty treat they can find in your kitchen. Fruit and sweets are good, but they'll also eat pet food, dairy items, or pretty much anything else they can find.

Count the Colony

Stink ants can live in colonies of 100,000! This one has far fewer. Count (or guess!) how many stink ants are here.

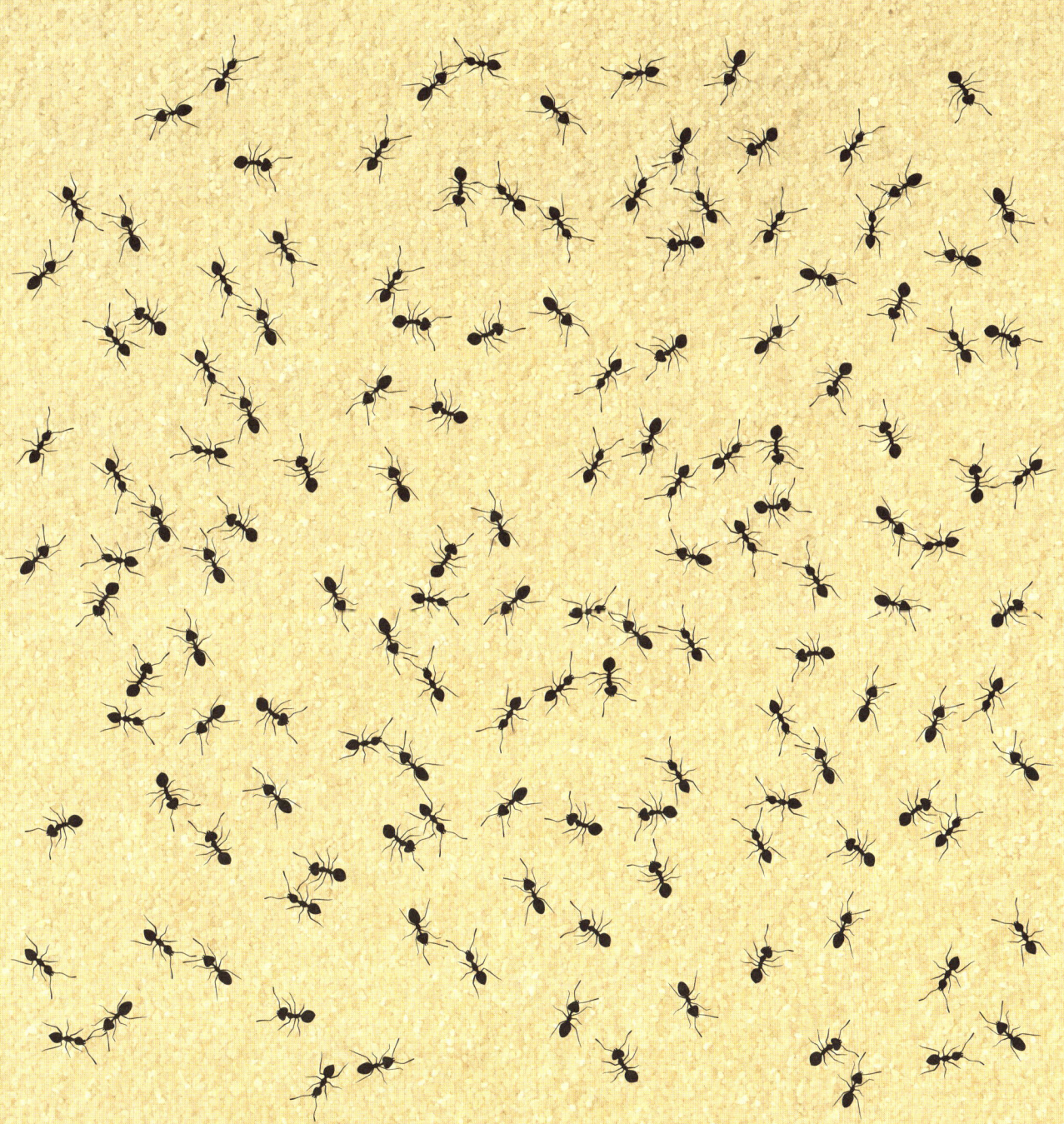

Pretty Gross

Here's a peek at the some of the prettiest bugs that are also gross!

The **Picasso bug**'s markings look like a gorgeous, colorful work of art. These little masterpieces are only about 0.5 inches (1.6 cm). But watch out—they have a smelly side! Picasso bugs are a type of stink bug. **P.U.!**

Is that a stunning jewel glinting in the sun? No, it's a **cuckoo wasp**. This bug looks like an emerald with wings, but its behavior isn't nearly as lovely as its appearance. Cuckoo wasps sneak into other insects' nests when they're not there and lay their own eggs. Their larvae eat the nest owners' eggs once they hatch. Not so nice!

The **orchid mantis** uses its pretty looks to hunt! Its flowery appearance lures in bugs in search of pollen and nectar. When those bugs get close enough, the orchid mantis attacks with sharp legs.

The colorful **rainbow milkweed locust** lives in Madagascar, where it feeds on the milkweed plant. That plant allows them to be deadly: When in danger, the rainbow milkweed locust creates a froth under its wings that's made of toxins from the milkweed plant.

Picasso Bug

Cuckoo Wasp

I'll be your best bud!

Orchid Mantis

Rainbow Milkweed Locust

Beautiful Bugs

Color in these beautiful and gross bugs.

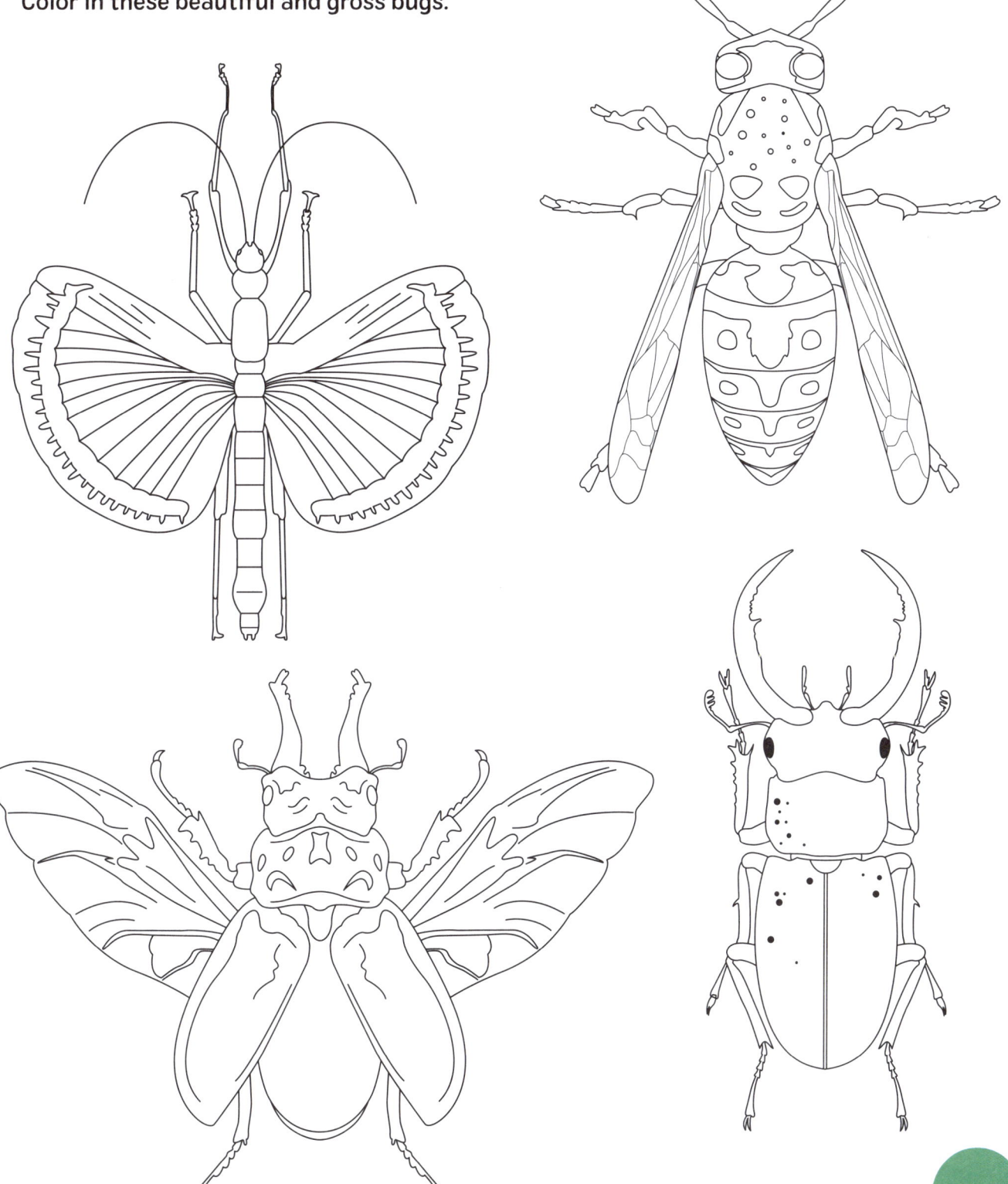

On the Fly

HOUSEFLY

Houseflies might just be the grossest bugs ever!

Here are just a few facts about them and their **disgusting behaviors**:

- They vomit on food before they eat it. They don't have teeth and can't chew, so **barfing on food** helps break it down so they can slurp it up.
- They eat **garbage**. Decaying, wet stuff is just too tempting.
- They defecate (that means **poop**) all the time. Some researchers think that they do it each time they land.
- Their taste receptors (like buds) are **on their feet**. Mmm, delicious!
- They're **covered in germs** because of all the time they spend on poop, rotting things, and dead things.

Even more gross than all that? Unfortunately they don't only like dead and rotten stuff, **they also like the food we eat**. Remember all their unlovely behaviors next time you find one sitting in the potato salad at your next picnic!

Gross-Out Meter

Color in how gross you think this bug is.

Add the Flies!

Draw the flies into this scene. Where do you think their favorite spots would be?

Unlovely Larvae
MAGGOTS

How about a hug?

If you think houseflies are gross, just wait till you meet their babies.

Maggots are baby flies (**larvae**), creatures so gross that Hollywood has made movies about giant, human-eating ones (don't worry, real maggots are tiny!). Here's how housefly larvae come into the world: Their creepy fly moms lay eggs in disgusting things like **rotting food**, **dead animals**, and **poop**. That's where they are born. If you've ever seen what look like white rice grains moving, you've discovered maggots!

SICKENING SCALE
How slimy, creepy, stinky is this bug?
Color in your rating.

CREEPY ✿ ✿ ✿ ✿ ✿
STINKY ✿ ✿ ✿ ✿ ✿
CRAWLY ✿ ✿ ✿ ✿ ✿
SLIMY ✿ ✿ ✿ ✿ ✿
HAIRY ✿ ✿ ✿ ✿ ✿
HUGE ✿ ✿ ✿ ✿ ✿

Little Itty-Bitty Icky Babies

Flies have a creepy but interesting life cycle. Think about the creepy bug you made up on page 25. Now draw its life cycle.

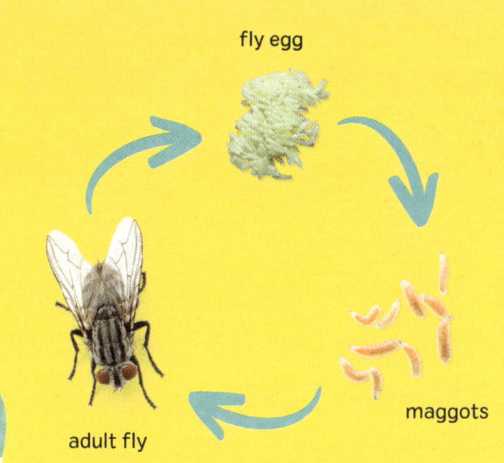

fly egg

maggots

adult fly

A Fly's Life Cycle

Creepy Bloodsuckers

What do fleas, ticks, and lice all have in common?

They survive by eating . . . **you**! *Shudder.* These creatures are **out for blood**.

Fleas

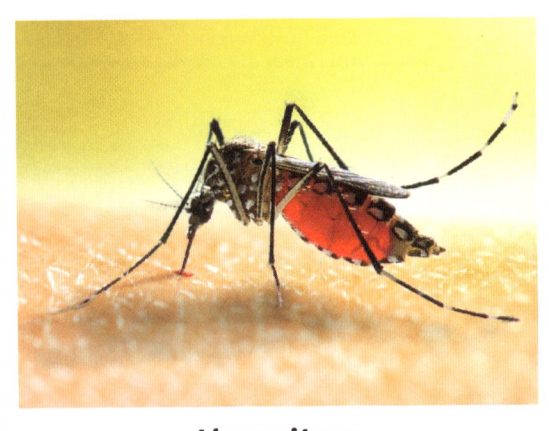
Mosquitoes

Lice

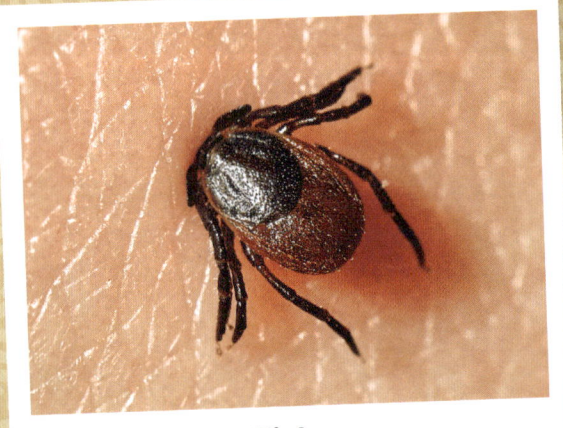
Ticks

Horseflies

Fill in the Facts

Find out more about these vampires of the insect world by unscrambling the answers below.

You look delicious!

Fleas

These pests often get a ride into your home on your furry friends, your ___ (ODG) or ___ (TAC). Fleas don't fly, but they can ____ (UMPJ)! In fact, they can leap with one ____ (OOFT) into the air.

Find: DOG, CAT, JUMP, FOOT

Mosquitoes

Only the _____ (FLAMEE) mosquitoes drink blood; the males eat fruit and nectar. These bugs have been around for 120 _____ (LIMLINO) years!

Find: FEMALE, MILLION

Lice

Lice eggs are called ____ (SNIT). Female lice can lay up to 10 eggs each day, sticking them to a person's ____ (RAIH). They make your head _____ (YTCIH).

Find: NITS, HAIR, ITCHY

Ticks

Though often considered bugs, these eight-legged bloodsuckers are actually _____ (AARCNISDH), related to spiders. Ticks spread _____ (SGREM) and diseases.

Find: ARACHNIDS, GERMS

Horseflies

Ouch! That ____ (URHT)! Painful horsefly bites leave red _____ (MUBPS). These flies have special, spongy mouths that soak up _____ (OODLB). In addition to humans, a favorite food source is _____ (SORSHE), where they get their name.

Find: HURT, BUMPS, BLOOD, HORSES

What a Bug!
WĒTĀPUNGA

These insects have been around for **190 MILLION** years, but they're now endangered and protected by the New Zealand government.

You know a bug is going to gross you out when its Māori name translates to "god of ugly things"!

The **giant** wētā, or wētāpunga, isn't just the **ugliest** bug in New Zealand. It also gets the top prize in a few other competitions. **Heaviest** bug in the world? Winner: wētāpunga. (It weighs about as much as a small bird.) Biggest **poop** of any **invertebrate**? Winner again: wētāpunga. (Their poop is about a half inch, or 1.3 cm long.) But don't let their size, name, and looks fool you. Wētāpungas are **gentle** giant bugs. They don't sting, inject venom, or bite. These **herbivores** mostly hide in leaves on the forest floor, slowly chomping their way through **plants**.

Gross-Out Meter

Color in how gross you think this bug is.

Find the Wētā Words

Find the bold words in the word search.

```
G  I  N  N  N  T  G  G  I  B  S  S  N  S  L
G  H  S  N  S  P  V  N  T  H  S  S  E  S  R
I  R  E  R  E  E  L  I  R  S  P  R  P  P  P
A  L  N  E  L  B  N  G  I  S  P  I  N  L  S
N  E  E  L  T  S  S  H  V  S  S  H  S  S  S
T  V  I  T  O  A  P  O  O  P  E  I  T  B  T
E  T  G  N  E  T  R  T  B  A  L  A  H  S  N
T  B  S  E  T  B  S  B  V  S  S  I  E  H  A
I  E  E  G  I  E  P  I  E  I  G  H  S  T  L
L  E  I  S  I  T  E  S  E  T  T  I  L  O  P
B  S  I  L  E  S  T  L  A  T  R  G  S  S  H
A  E  G  I  T  T  T  I  E  I  B  E  L  G  N
S  U  U  N  P  T  T  E  E  S  S  S  V  A  I
N  N  N  T  O  N  N  T  H  S  H  P  E  N  B
S  P  H  E  R  B  I  V  O  R  E  S  A  G  I
```

gentle	**hissing**	**ugliest**
giant	**plants**	**invertebrate**
heaviest	**poop**	**herbivores**

Pile It On

Imagine sticking dead bugs all over yourself. That's what these bugs do.

Meet *Acanthaspis petax*. It's a type of assassin bug. Sure, we know assassin bugs are gross in general (see page 32), but these insects are next level. After they hunt like most assassin bugs do, it gets grosser: *Acanthaspis* stacks the lifeless bodies of its prey on its back. Those bodies stay there, and pile up, thanks to a sticky substance on their exoskeletons. Creepy? Yes. Disgusting? Totally.

They're not the only bugs that cover themselves in gross stuff. The **aphid lion**, also known as the **junk bug**, is the larva of the green lacewing. It dresses up in dead aphids, plus bits of leaves and lichens. The **masked hunter bug** covers itself in so much dust, lint, and dirt that it looks like a fluffy gray puff with antennas. **Larval caddisflies** use silk to attach leaves, stems, and pretty much anything else they find (like tiny snail shells) to themselves.

This behavior is called self-decoration, and it's a way that bugs and other creatures (like crabs) hide themselves from predators. Researchers think that it might also protect them once they're spotted: A predator attempting a bite gets a mouthful of gross stuff instead of the actual bug underneath.

Acanthaspis petax

Aphid lion

Masked hunter bug

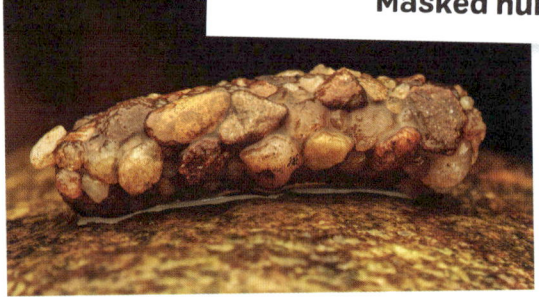

Larval caddisflies

DIY Decorations

This bug needs some camouflage. Draw on sticks, leaves, other bugs, bits of fluff, or anything else you think would help it hide from predators.

Don't Sweat It

SCORPION FLY

Scorpion flies look and sound terrifying!

Scorpion flies belong to **MECOPTERA**, a group of bugs that first appeared more than **250 MILLION YEARS AGO**.

SICKENING SCALE

How slimy, creepy, stinky is this bug? Color in your rating.

CREEPY ✿ ✿ ✿ ✿ ✿

STINKY ✿ ✿ ✿ ✿ ✿

CRAWLY ✿ ✿ ✿ ✿ ✿

SLIMY ✿ ✿ ✿ ✿ ✿

HAIRY ✿ ✿ ✿ ✿ ✿

HUGE ✿ ✿ ✿ ✿ ✿

They have a curled scorpion tail and a big, scary mouth. But it's what these fearsome flies drink that is really horrifying: your SWEAT! Ewwww! While they aren't looking to drink your blood, scorpion flies *do* have a taste for dead things: they eat dead insects and steal prey from spiderwebs. While they *love* to **lick your sweat**, these creepy-crawlies are actually pretty harmless to people. That **fearsome tail** contains no stinger. They're not venomous, they hang out in gardens, and they're thought to be distantly related to butterflies.

Fearsome Fly!

Doodle your own scary-looking fly. Borrow features from other fearsome creatures. The mane of a lion? The teeth of a shark? The trilling tail of a rattlesnake?

My fly's name: _____

What it eats: _____

Where it lives: _____

The Big Bad Behemoth

GOLIATH BIRDEATER

The birdeater's venom stops its prey from moving and **LIQUEFIES ITS INSIDES** (yum!).

If you have a fear of spiders, you might want to turn the page!

Meet the biggest spider in the world: the **goliath birdeater**. It can grow as big as a dinner plate. But its size isn't the only gross thing about it. The goliath birdeater is **hairy**.

So hairy, in fact, it's got hair to spare—if it's under attack, it rubs its hair in a way that makes a scary hissing sound, and then it can **throw hair** at its foes. It also has fangs tucked away until it's ready to use them.

These spiders use their fangs to inject venom into their prey. They then drag their prey into their den and suck out its guts.

Sure, they eat birds—but only sometimes. The goliath birdeater also hunts mice, frogs, and other insects. Just thinking about a spider **big enough to eat a mouse** is enough to give you chills!

Gross-Out Meter

Color in how gross you think this bug is.

How Big???

This spider is the size of a goliath birdeater. Trace your hand over it to compare its size to yours. Can you imagine holding one? Now, color in your spider.

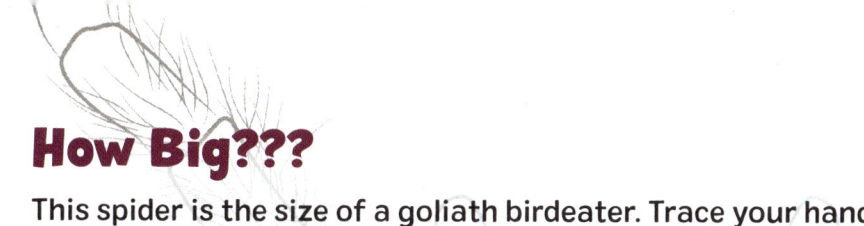

Wait, *How* Do Bees Make Honey?

HONEYBEE

Busy buzzing bees flit from flower to flower.

They're working hard to collect **nectar**. But how does that flower nectar turn into the sweet, delicious, gooey **honey** that's in your kitchen? Well, we've got some gross news for you. To get that nectar back to their hive, the bee has to drink it. When the bee arrives at the hive, it throws up the honey into the mouth of a waiting bee. Then *that* bee crawls into the hive and **pukes** the nectar into the honeycomb. Bees store nectar in their crops—**special pouches** that are kind of like stomachs but don't do any actual digesting.

SICKENING SCALE

How slimy, creepy, stinky is this bug?
Color in your rating.

CREEPY
STINKY
CRAWLY
SLIMY
HAIRY
HUGE

Searcher Bee

Be a searcher bee and find the honey-making words in the hive below.

```
Y L N P R R H R O E B A I O P
F B R P O R C E C Y Z O H O W
N H O U R C R E H R R C C O Y
M F T R E A H O N E Y C O M B
R Y E N P L T Y F H C W B Y
O V N O H R E C O L P O E U O
F N O C B E E L E R O A E E O
N Z E E O B E C B N Z W R H E
A A E G A G R Y A O F Z E N U
I V Y B H C E O E H L Y B R A
T R Y Y F O H O E R I U I P R
O N E N O P O N O C Z V E E C
O Z F G H N Z A E Z C E E Y O
A P F M E R H F H Z U N B O O
N H O G Z E Z N E N G L P R I
```

crop   hive   honeycomb   buzz

nectar   fan   flower   gooey

Who's the GROSSEST?

Look back on your Sickening Scales and Gross-Out Meters and think about every bug in the book. Now, rank each bug 1–38, with #1 being the most disgusting. Crown the winner—the grossest, most sickening bug in this book—on page 74!

Stink Bug

Rank _____

Bombardier Beetle

Rank _____

Dung Beetle

Rank _____

Spittlebug

Rank _____

Earwig

Rank _____

Hercules Beetle

Rank _____

Camel Spider

Rank _____

Tarantula

Rank _____

Monkey Slug Caterpillar

Rank _____

Millipede

Rank _____

Assassin Bug

Rank _____

Stick Bug

Rank _____

Bedbug

Rank _____

Weevil

Rank _____

Pear Slug

Rank _____

Cockroach

Rank _____

Glowworm

Rank _____

Bird Poop Caterpillar

Rank _____

Stink Ant

Rank _____

Picasso Bug

Rank _____

Cuckoo Wasp

Rank _____

Orchid Mantis

Rank _____

Rainbow Milkweed Locust

Rank _____

Housefly

Rank _____

Maggot

Rank _____

Flea

Rank _____

Mosquito

Rank _____

Lice

Rank _____

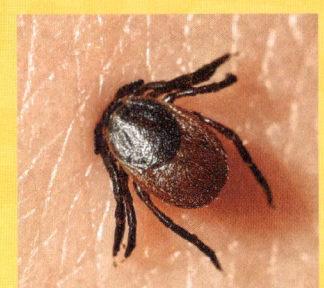

Tick

Rank _____

Horsefly

Rank _____

Wētāpunga

Rank _____

Acanthaspis petax

Rank _____

Aphid Lion

Rank _____

Masked Hunter Bug

Rank _____

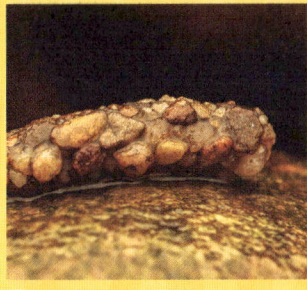

Larval Caddisfly

Rank _____

Scorpion Fly

Rank _____

Honeybee

Rank _____

Goliath Birdeater

Rank _____

The grossest bug is:

_____

draw your winner here

ANSWER KEY

Page 9

The insects are: Ant, Wasp, Butterfly, Caterpillar, Glowworm, Walking Stick.

Banana slugs are mollusks. Daddy longlegs are a type of arachnid called a mollusk. A spider is an arachnid.

Page 15

Ant vs Beetle: Beetle wins because its chemical burn hurts or kills the ant.

Toad vs Beetle: Beetle wins because toads swallow the bugs whole, which means that inside the toad's stomach, the bombardier beetle can fire its painful blast—the toad spits up the beetle, and the beetle survives.

Bird vs Beetle: The bird wins because it's bigger and its beak spears and wounds the beetle before swallowing it down.

Page 17

Page 21

House spiders: These creepy-crawlies spin webs to catch mosquitoes, cockroaches, and wasps.

Hoverflies: These yellow jacket look-alikes don't sting and are also great pollinators.

Herder ants: These insects protect aphids from predators. In exchange, the aphids feed them a sugary substance called honeydew.

House centipedes: These many-legged hunters feast on pests in your pantry.

Page 23

These hairy larvae grow up to be snug bugs in rugs. **Carpet beetle**

Rat-tailed maggots get their name because of their tails. **Drone fly**

Grown, these flies look like another insect. **Hoverfly**

Though they begin their lives as white wormlike larvae, these insects grow up to be black or reddish brown. **Black ant**

Page 27

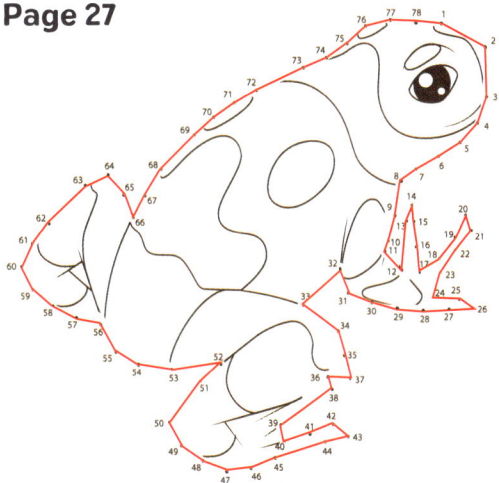

Page 31

Tractor millipede: 300 legs
Red millipede: 750 legs
Flat-backed millipede: 40 legs
Giant pill millipede: 42 legs
Giant millipede: 160 legs
Pink dragon millipede: 24 legs

Page 35

Page 37

Spider Beetle: What's alike? Coloring, antenna.
What's different? Body shape, leg shape, face.

Tick: What's alike? Coloring, head.
What's different? Number of legs, body shape.

Cockroach Nymph: What's alike? Coloring.
What's different? Body shape, leg shape,
antenna, head.

Carpet Beetle: What's alike? Coloring, antenna.
What's different? Body shape, leg shape, head.

Page 39

Page 41

Page 43

Page 49

Page 45

Domino, Hissing, Australian, Death's Head

Page 47

Page 51

143 ants

Page 59

Fleas: These pests often get a ride into your home on your furry friends, your **DOG** or **CAT**. Fleas don't fly, but they can **JUMP**! In fact, they can leap with one **FOOT** in the air.

Mosquitoes: Only the **FEMALE** mosquitoes drink blood; the males eat fruit and nectar. These bugs have been around for 120 **MILLION** years!

Lice: Lice eggs are called **NITS**. Female lice can lay up to 10 eggs each day, sticking them to a person's **HAIR**. They make your head **ITCHY**.

Ticks: Though often considered bugs, these eight-legged bloodsuckers are actually **ARACHNIDS**, related to spiders. Ticks spread **GERMS** and diseases.

Horseflies: Ouch! That **HURT**! Painful horsefly bites leave red **BUMPS**. These flies have special, spongy mouths that soak up **BLOOD**. In addition to humans, a favorite food source is **HORSES**, where they get their name.

Page 61

Page 69

Glossary

abdomen: The part of an insect behind the thorax.

bug: An insect or a creepy-crawly critter.

camouflage: The ability to hide, disguise, or blend into the background.

dung: An animal's waste, or manure (also known as poop!).

exoskeleton: A hard outer shell that protects the body underneath; an "outside skeleton."

gross: Disgusting, yucky, sickening, hideous, icky, nasty, or foul.

larva: A newly hatched baby bug; larvae (more than one larva) usually look like worms and don't have wings.

molt: To shed.

nymph: A young insect; nymphs often look different from their grown-up form.

osmeterium: A gland in a caterpillar that gives off a stinky smell when the creature is threatened.

predator: A creature that hunts and eats prey.

prey: A creature that's hunted and eaten by a predator.

proboscis: A long, usually tubelike mouth part for sucking.

species: A group of closely related plants or animals that can reproduce.

thorax: The middle part of an insect's body, behind the head and before the abdomen.

toxin: A substance a creature makes that's poisonous, or even deadly, to other creatures.

Image Credits

(SS=Shutterstock, WC=Wikimedia Commons)

Front cover (top [...] 67/SS; front cover (left), zerbor/SS; front cover (top right), Eric Isselee/SS; front cover (bottom),Tran The Ngoc/SS; [...] op left),Kurit afshen/SS; back cover (bottom left),KangGod/SS; back cover (top right), Macronatura. es/SS; bac[...] ght),Melinda Fawver/SS; 1 (top left), Kurit afshen/SS; 1 (top right), Macronatura.es/SS; 1 (bottom), Nynke van H[...] SUTTIPON YAKHAM/SS; 3, watchara panyajun/SS; 4, Chanasorn Charuthas/SS; 5, Somyot Mali-ngam/ SS; 6 (clockwis[...] op left), David Havel/SS; photochem_PA/Flickr; DoreenB Photography/SS; AgriTech/SS; 7 (left), Rosadi adi/ SS; 7 (right),KRIA[...] O OLEKSII/SS; 8, Eric Isselee/SS; 9 (top, left to right), HWall/SS; Abudzaky/SS; Luc Pouliot/SS; 9 (center, left to right), Yeung Man Chun/SS; Darkdiamond67/SS; Joseph Scott Photography/SS; 9 (bottom, left to right), ZB creation/SS; Egor Kamelev/Pexels; Darkdiamond67/SS; 10, axeiz/SS; 11 (gnat),Roblan/SS; 11 (bee), xpixel/SS; 11 (grasshopper), HHelene/SS; 11 (wasp), unpict/SS; 11 (pill bug), kungfu01/SS; 11 (butterfly), Soho A Studio/SS; 11 (ant),Peter Togel/SS; 11 (praying mantis), Olhastock/SS; 11 (moth),Melinda Fawver/SS; 11 (fly), Eric Isselee/SS; 11 (cricket) prapann/SS; 12, Jenn Forman Orth/Flickr; 13 (trash), P.Cartwright/ SS; 13 (milk) 9foto/SS;13 (skunk), BB Outdoors/SS; 13 (shoes), CMG_IG/SS; 13 (stinkbug), photochem_PA/Flickr; 13 (dog),woodHunt/ SS; 14, pryzmat/SS; 15 (left), stevenku/SS; 15 (center), ,Katja Schulz/Flickr; 15 (right),Warren Metcalf/SS; 15 (bottom), fercast/SS; 16, Henk Bogaard/SS; 17 (possum), IrinaK/SS; 17 (earwig),kungfu01/SS; 17 (white bird),Dino Stocks/SS; 17 (raven), WildlifeWorld/ SS; 17 (dung beetle), Henk Bogaard/SS; 18, David Havel/SS; 18 (bottom), John Moorby/SS; 19, Macronatura.es/SS; 20, jackcinde/ SS; 21 (top to bottom), HHelene/SS; Andrey Pavlov/SS; photomaster/SS; Rudmer Zwerve/SS; 22 (top), ran dunu samaranayaka/ SS; 22 (bottom), Nick626/SS; 23 (clockwise from top left), Henrik Larsson/SS; Macronatura.es/SS; Dreamland Photography/SS; Tomasz Klejdysz/SS; Wirestock Creators/SS; Tomasz Klejdysz/SS; Victor Suarez Naranjo/SS; Tomasz Klejdysz/SS; 24, Dmitry Fch/SS; 25 (clockwise from top left), Robcartorres/SS; SS; frank60/SS; Cornel Constantin/SS; chinahbzyg/SS; feeling lucky/ SS; CHEN HSI FU/SS; guraydere/SS; 26, reptiles4all/SS; 27 (top), Nynke van Holten/SS; 27 (bottom), Kurit afshen/SS; 28, Geraldo Morais/SS; 29 (left), zerbor/SS; 29 (right), Cosmin Mancy/SS; 30, Piyapong pc/SS; 31(top right), Sakdinon Kadchiangsaen/SS; 31 (clockwise from top left), Charles J. Sharp/WC; Dan Olsen/SS; Beautifiers/SS; tee262/SS; Abdul Gapur Dayak/SS; AgriTech/ SS; 32, Georgi Baird/SS; 33 (top to bottom), Nasrul_hakiiiim/SS; Karakking/SS; Steve Lovegrove/SS; 34 (top), Space creator/SS; 34, Mark Brandon/SS; 35 (Clockwise from top left), Nikolas Gregor/SS; KarSol/SS; Esin Deniz/SS; Pepew Fegley/SS; Dr.MYM/SS; Lost_in_the_Midwest/SS; TinoFotografie/SS; 37 (clockwise from top left), Tomasz Klejdysz/SS; MagicBloods/SS; Tomasz Klejdysz/ SS; bamgraphy/SS; 38, Rasmuscool99/SS; 38 (right),Artush/SS; 39, m.malinika/SS; 40, IanRedding/SS; 40 (right), Simon Grove ; 41 (clockwise from top left), Muddy knees/SS; chinahbzyg/SS; Muddy knees/SS; elmuzastudio/SS; Hrushkovyk/SS; rsooll/SS; 42, nujames10/SS; 43 (clockwise from top left), Vitalii Hulai/SS; Gabriel Dominella/SS; Vinicius R. Souza/SS; Rebel Red Runner/SS; samray/SS; Karla Guerrero Carrillo/SS; Robert Adami/SS; Mark_Kostich/SS; 44, luis2499/SS; 45 (top right), watchara panyajun/ SS; 45 (left, top to bottom), desertnaturalist/ArtMediaFactory/SS; Artush/SS; K Hanley CHDPhoto/SS; 46 (top), Shaun Jeffers/ SS; 46 (right), Pchelovek1205/WC; 47, Melinda Fawver/SS; 48, Brian Lasenby/SS; 48 (right), Mirek Kijewski/SS; 49 (clockwise from top left), LMPark Photo/SS; Kevin Collison/SS; Cathy Keifer/SS; Nikolay Kurzenko/SS; Brett Hondow/SS; Cathy Keifer/SS; Judson Castro/SS; Alexander Sviridov/SS; 50, Wirestock Creators/SS; 52 (top to bottom), A. Kehinde/SS; Chui Wui Jing/SS; Kurit afshen/ SS; Artush/SS; 54, nechaevkon/SS; 55, Firsova Kateryna/SS; 56, O_Solara/SS; 56 (right), Ethan Quinn/SS; 57 (eggs), monster_code/ SS; 57 (maggots), Nick N A/SS; 57 (fly), Nataliia K/SS; 58 (clockwise from top right), Tomasz Klejdysz/SS; Protasov AN/SS; achkin/ SS; Evgeniyqw/SS; Gulf MG/SS; 59, Melinda Fawver/SS; 60, Kim Howell/SS; 60 (right), Danny Ye/SS; 62 (top to bottom), Joyce LCY/ SS; chinahbzyg/SS; D. Kucharski K. Kucharska/SS; JP.Chromosphaera/SS; 64, epioxi/SS; 66, Milan Zygmunt/SS; 68, chinahbzyg/SS; 70 (clockwise from top left), Jenn Forman Orth/Flickr; pryzmat/SS; David Havel/SS; ran dunu samaranayaka/SS; reptiles4all/SS; Dmitry Fch/SS; jackcinde/SS; Henk Bogaard/SS; 71 (clockwise from top left), Geraldo Morais/SS; Piyapong pc/SS; Space creator/ SS; Rasmuscool99/SS; luis2499/SS; Brian Lasenby/SS; Pchelovek1205/WC; IanRedding/SS; TinoFotografie/SS; Georgi Baird/SS; 72 (clockwise from top left), Wirestock Creators/SS; A. Kehinde/SS; Kurit afshen/SS; nechaevkon/SS; Tomasz Klejdysz/SS; Protasov AN/SS; Gulf MG/SS; Ethan Quinn/SS; Artush/SS; Chui Wui Jing/SS; 73 (clockwise from top left), Evgeniyqw/SS; achkin/SS; Joyce LCY/SS; D. Kucharski K. Kucharska/SS; epioxi/SS; Milan Zygmunt/SS; chinahbzyg/SS; JP.Chromosphaera/SS; chinahbzyg/SS; Kim Howell/SS; 78, KangGod/SS; 79, cynoclub/SS; 80, Mr. SUTTIPON YAKHAM/SS